D1538237

Extreme Mountain Biking Moves

By Kathleen W. Deady

Consultant:
Eric Moore
National Events Director
National Off-Road Bicycle Association
(NORBA)

CAPSTONE
HIGH-INTEREST
BOOKS

an imprint of Capstone Press
Mankato, Minnesota

Capstone High-Interest Books are published by Capstone Press
151 Good Counsel Drive, P.O. Box 669, Mankato, Minnesota 56002
http://www.capstone-press.com

Library of Congress Cataloging-in-Publication Data
Deady, Kathleen W.
    Extreme mountain biking moves/by Kathleen W. Deady.
    p. cm.—(Behind the moves)
    Summary: Discusses the sport of mountain biking, describing some of the racing
and trick moves as well as safety concerns.
    Includes bibliographical references (p. 31) and index.
    ISBN 0-7368-1513-9
    1. All terrain cycling—Juvenile literature. 2. Extreme sports—Juvenile literature.
[1. All terrain cycling. 2. Extreme sports.] I. Title. II. Series.
GV1056 .D43 2003
796.6'3—dc21   2002008179

Editorial Credits
Carrie Braulick, editor; Karen Risch, product planning editor; Kia Adams,
    series designer; Molly Nei, book designer; Jo Miller, photo researcher

Photo Credits
Corbis/Duomo, cover, 24; Gunter Marx Photography, 10; Kevin R. Morris, 12;
    David Stoeklein, 13; Lee Cohen, 14; Karl Weatherly, 22, 27 (top); Mark A.
    Johnson, 24
Getty Images/Jeff Gross, 4 (inset), 24 (inset); Mike Powell, 7, 10 (inset); Robert Laberge,
    27 (bottom), 28
Image Finders/Mark E. Gibson, 8
Photo Network/Art Brewer, 4; Tony Demin, 21
PhotoDisc, Inc., 16 (inset)
Photri-Microstock, 19
Viesti Collection, Inc./Dan Peha, 16

Table of Contents

Chapter One: Extreme Mountain Biking 5

Chapter Two: Racing Moves 11

Chapter Three: Advanced Moves .. 17

Chapter Four: Safety 25

Extreme Mountain Biking Slang 23

Words to Know 30

To Learn More 31

Useful Addresses 31

Internet Sites 32

Index 32

Mountain bikes are built for off-road areas.

Learn about:

Mountain bike history

Design of mountain bikes

Mountain bike racing

Extreme Mountain Biking

In July 2002, Alison Dunlap was racing in the women's cross-country race of the Telluride 360 Degree Festival in Telluride, Colorado. As she neared the finish line, Argentinian racer Jimena Florit was right behind her. Dunlap worked to keep her lead. She finished 48 seconds before Florit and won the race.

Alison Dunlap is one of the best cross-country mountain bikers in the United States. In 2001, she won the women's World Mountain Bike Cross-Country Championships. She won the gold medal for mountain biking in the 1999 Pan-American Games. Dunlap also has competed in the Olympics.

The First Mountain Bikes

In the 1970s, some riders wanted a bike they could ride on mountain trails. At that time, bike manufacturers did not produce bikes that could handle rough mountain terrain. BMX bikes could travel over rough ground, but they were small and had only one gear. Ten-speed bikes were for street riding. They were not strong enough to handle off-road areas.

The first mountain bikes were built in the late 1970s. These bikes had strong frames, wide tires, and 18 gears. People could ride these bikes in rough, off-road areas. By the mid-1980s, bike manufacturers produced and sold thousands of mountain bikes.

Mountain Bike Features

Mountain bikes are equipped to travel over rough terrain. Most bikes have frames made of aluminum or titanium. These metals are strong and lightweight. Mountain bike tires have bumps called knobbies. The knobbies grip the ground to produce traction. Traction prevents the bikes from slipping on loose terrain.

Mountain bikes have both front and rear cantilever brakes. These strong brakes with thick

cables help slow down the bikes. The brakes also help riders control their bikes during tricks.

Most mountain bikes have 15 to 27 gears. Riders can shift gears according to their riding surface. They use low gears to travel uphill. They use high gears to travel downhill.

Mountain bike tires produce good traction on loose terrain.

Riders zig-zag around poles in slalom races.

Types of Extreme Mountain Biking

Some people ride mountain bikes just for fun or exercise. For others, mountain biking is an extreme sport. Some extreme mountain bikers participate in races. Others ride through obstacle courses or perform difficult stunts.

Extreme mountain bikers can compete in various races. They may compete in dual slalom races. In these races, two riders race against each other on short downhill courses marked by poles. Cross-country race courses have many natural obstacles such as dirt mounds, rocky paths, streams, and mudholes. Downhill racers travel down mountains through courses with natural and artificial obstacles. Racers can reach speeds of more than 60 miles (97 kilometers) per hour on these courses. Uphill racers travel up steep slopes. Endurance races are long-distance races that may last several days.

Some extreme mountain bikers compete in trials competitions. These riders must travel over obstacles without putting a foot down. Riders receive a point if a foot touches the ground. The rider with the fewest number of points wins the event.

Mountain bike racers have advanced skills.

Learn about:

- *Downhill racing*

- *Uphill racing*

- *Turning corners*

Chapter Two

Racing Moves

Extreme mountain bike racers have learned basic skills. They can easily shift gears and brake. They know how to move their weight to stay balanced. Most racers also have developed advanced skills. These skills help racers travel quickly while controlling their bikes.

Downhill Racing Skills

Downhill racers need to handle their bikes down steep slopes at high speeds. They shift into high gears. Downhill racers crouch low on their bikes and move their weight back. This position helps prevent them from flying forward if they hit an object.

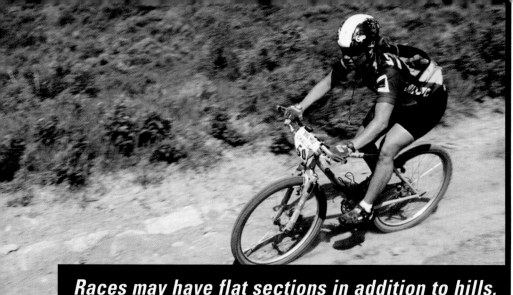

Races may have flat sections in addition to hills.

Downhill racers usually use their front and rear brakes together. They feather the brakes by lightly squeezing and releasing them. Feathering controls the bike's speed without locking up the brakes. Riders who lock up the brakes can easily skid out of control.

Uphill Racing Skills

Uphill racers shift into low gears to make pedaling easier. They try to keep an even speed. Uphill racers move their weight forward. They keep their head close to the handlebars to keep the front wheel on the ground. Uphill racers sometimes pull back on the handlebars during each pedal stroke. This movement helps keep the rear wheel on the ground.

Uphill racers may stand to ride up short, steep hills. They sometimes pull themselves toward the handlebars during each downward pedal stroke. This movement helps racers increase power to travel faster up steep slopes.

Uphill racers may stand to ride up steep hills.

Singletracks have room for only one bike.

Turning and Singletracks

Mountain bike racers need to turn corners properly. They brake to slow down before they reach a curve. Braking helps prevent skidding. Racers also look and lean in the direction of the turn. They ride to the outside of sharp turns to stay balanced.

In loose terrain, racers move their weight forward as they turn corners. The front wheel then has better traction. Racers also push down on the outside handlebar and pedal to keep their bikes upright through the curve.

Racers sometimes ride on very narrow trails called singletracks. They slow down, look ahead, and control their bikes carefully on these paths. Rocks, logs, and other objects sometimes block singletracks.

Wheelies are a popular type of advanced move.

Harris Park
Loop #2

ELEVATION - 9900 FEET
DISTANCE - 4.2 MILES
VERTICAL - 550 FEET

DISTANCE - 2.7 MILES
VERTICAL - 300 FEET

Elbert Creek
Road Loop #4 ◆
ADVANCED

ELEVATION - 10,700 FEET
DISTANCE - 10 MILES
VERTICAL - 850 FEET

Goo Creek
Loop #5

ELEVAT... 100 FEET
DIST... 4.3 MILES
VE... - 300 FEET

Hermosa Cliff #7
Overlook

FOLLOW MAIN ROAD

ELEVATION - 10,480 FEET
DISTANCE - 9 MILES
VERTICAL - 550 FEET

Learn about:

■ *Jumping objects*

■ *Changing directions*

■ *Stunts*

Advanced Moves

Extreme mountain bikers sometimes perform advanced moves. These moves can help them get around or over obstacles. Riders also do advanced moves to turn quickly or to perform stunts.

Bunny Hops and Wheelies

Extreme mountain bikers often perform bunny hops. The rider crouches low on the bike. The rider then stands and lifts up on the handlebars. Both wheels come off the ground together. Riders can do bunny hops while moving or standing in place.

Riders perform bunny hops for various reasons. They usually perform bunny hops to jump over objects. They also do bunny hops to lift their bikes onto obstacles. Some riders do sideways bunny hops to jump out of ditches or ruts.

Extreme mountain bikers sometimes do wheelies to jump over objects. The rider slides backward and pulls up on the handlebars. The front wheel of the bike then lifts into the air. The rider continues to pedal while balancing on the back wheel. The rider slides forward after the front wheel is over the object. The back wheel then rolls over the object.

Tailwhips and Kick Turns

Riders sometimes need to turn sharply. They may perform a tailwhip while traveling downhill. The rider first applies the front brake. The rear wheel then lifts. The rider balances on the front wheel and pulls the rear end around. The rider then begins traveling in the opposite direction.

Riders can perform kick turns while traveling uphill. Kick turns are similar to

tailwhips. Riders perform kick turns while balancing on the rear wheel instead of the front wheel. Riders apply the rear brake and pull the bike's front end up. They then pull the front wheel around to travel in the opposite direction.

Both wheels come off the ground during a

Other Moves

Extreme mountain bikers also perform stunts. They may hop their bikes sideways. They may do tabletops or tweaks in the air. To perform a tabletop, riders turn their handlebars and kick out the rear wheel in the same direction. Riders twist their handlebars back and forth in mid-air to do a tweak.

Riders may perform a trackstand. In this move, riders stop and balance on the pedals without putting their feet down on the ground. Racers sometimes perform trackstands to view their path.

Some extreme mountain bikers can perform front or rear pogos. The front pogo is one of the sport's most advanced moves. Riders lift the rear wheel. They then hop while balancing on the front wheel. To perform a rear pogo, riders perform a wheelie and hop.

Riders in trials competitions often perform drop-offs to get off high obstacles and onto the ground. Riders slowly pedal to the edge of the obstacle. They then do a

small wheelie and pedal off the obstacle. As the bike falls, riders stand to bring the bike's front end down. Riders try to land on the rear wheel to keep their bikes under control.

Riders twist the handlebars during tweaks.

Extreme Mountain Biking Slang

bacon—the scabs on a rider's elbows, knees, or other body parts

banana scraper—a low-hanging branch

biff—to crash

brain bucket—a helmet

death cookies—baseball-sized rocks on a trail

engine—a rider

gravity check—a fall off a bike

grinder—a long uphill climb

hammer—to ride fast and hard

steed—a mountain bike

superman—a rider who flies over the bike's handlebars

taco—a bent wheel

wash out—to have the front tire lose traction

Riders wear proper gear to prevent injuries.

Learn about:

Safety equipment

Safe riding rules

Mountain biking associations

Chapter Four

Safety

Extreme mountain bikers know that safety is important. They ride strong, properly equipped bikes. Riders make sure their bikes are well-maintained. They learn about how the parts of their bikes work. They check all parts for problems before each ride.

Safety Gear

A helmet is the most important piece of safety equipment. Helmets help protect a rider's head during crashes.

25

Downhill racers usually wear long-sleeved shirts and pants to protect themselves from scrapes and scratches. Cross-country racers often wear clothing made of material that absorbs moisture from the skin. This material helps keep riders dry and comfortable.

Riders wear other safety gear. Some riders wear pads to protect their knees and elbows. Most riders wear sport glasses to protect their eyes from the sun, branches, dust, and insects. Many mountain bikers also wear leather gloves to protect their hands and to help them grip the handlebars.

Mountain bikers carry some equipment for emergencies. They carry a small tool kit with items such as wrenches, screwdrivers, and a flat tire repair kit. They can use the tools to make emergency repairs. Mountain bikers also carry a first aid kit in case they become injured.

Safety Rules

Extreme mountain bikers follow safety guidelines. They look well ahead of where they are riding. They then can plan how to

avoid objects. Mountain bikers control the speed of their bikes. Downhill racers are especially cautious. These racers travel at high speeds. They are more likely to have serious crashes than other riders. Safe mountain bikers also know their skill level. They make sure they have mastered basic skills before performing advanced moves.

Safe mountain bikers follow other rules. They ride only where it is legal. They are careful not to damage trails. They try to ride with a partner. Another person can help them in an emergency.

Riders wear protective clothing to prevent scratches.

World Cup races often have difficult courses.

Organizations and Competitions

The popularity of mountain biking has caused many organizations to form. Many organizations maintain mountain biking trails. These organizations also encourage safe riding and require competitors to wear proper safety gear. In 1983, mountain bikers formed the National Off-Road Bicycle Association (NORBA). NORBA organizes more than 1,000 official mountain bike races each year. The International Mountain Bicycling Association (IMBA) creates and maintains mountain biking trails. The Canadian Cycling Association (CCA) organizes many races and maintains trails in Canada.

Both amateurs and professionals can take part in competitions. Professional racers usually have a license from an official organization. The licenses allow riders to compete in professional races. Amateurs do not have licenses. They often compete in local races. Some races allow both amateurs and professionals to compete.

Top mountain bike racers from around the world compete in many professional races. These races include the World Cup Series and the World Mountain Bike Championships.

Words to Know

feather (FE-thur)—to squeeze the brakes lightly and release them

frame (FRAYM)—the main body of a mountain bike

knobbies (NAW-beez)—the deep bumps on a tire that help the tire grip the ground

obstacle (OB-stuh-kuhl)—an object that stands in a mountain biker's way

rut (RUHT)—a deep, narrow track in the ground

singletrack (SING-guhl-trak)—a narrow trail wide enough for only one bike

skid (SKID)—to slide out of control

terrain (tur-RAYN)—the surface of the land

traction (TRAK-shuhn)—the gripping power that prevents a bike from slipping

To Learn More

Bizley, Kirk. *Mountain Biking.* Radical Sports. Chicago: Heinemann Library, 2000.

Mason, Paul. *Mountain Biking.* To the Limit. Austin, Texas: Raintree Steck-Vaughn, 2001.

Molzahn, Arlene Bourgeois. *Extreme Mountain Biking.* Extreme Sports. Mankato, Minn.: Capstone Press, 2000.

Useful Addresses

Canadian Cycling Association
702-2197 Riverside Drive
Ottawa, ON K1H 7X3
Canada

International Mountain Bicycling Association
1121 Broadway
Suite 203
Boulder, CO 80306

USA Cycling/NORBA
One Olympic Plaza
Colorado Springs, CO 80909-5775

Internet Sites

Track down many sites about mountain biking.
Visit the FACT HOUND at http://www.facthound.com

IT IS EASY! IT IS FUN!

1) Go to http://www.facthound.com
2) Type in: 0736815139
3) Click on "FETCH IT" and FACT HOUND will find
   several links hand-picked by our editors.

Relax and let our pal FACT HOUND do the research for you!

Index

bunny hops, 17–18

cross-country racing, 5, 9, 26, 29

downhill racing, 9, 11–12, 26, 27
drop-offs, 20
Dunlap, Alison, 5

gears, 6, 7, 11, 12

knobbies, 6

obstacle, 9, 15, 17, 18, 20, 21

pogo, 20

singletracks, 15

tabletops, 20
trackstand, 20
traction, 6, 15
trials competitions, 9, 20
tweak, 20

uphill racing, 9, 12–13

wheelie, 18, 20, 21